GAINING THE

COMMANDED BLESSINGS

By Dennis Paul Goldsworthy-Davis

Open Wells Ministries

15315 Capital Port

Sam Antonio, TX 78249

www.openwellsministries.org

Foreword by Bestselling Author

Robert Henderson

Open Wells Ministries International
15315 Capital Port
San Antonio, TX 78249

Library of Congress Number:

ISBN: 978-1-7355716-3-8

Printed in the United States of America
by Open Wells Ministries International

ACKNOWLEDGEMENTS

We have been shaped along the way and touched by so many. Bob Main was one who I saw such blessing on and then it had me search for what brought blessing. Chris Rodes has walked with me and encouraged me as a co-pastor of our church, Great Grace international. As I wrote a chapter he would read it and encourage.

Always Jeannie Hartman for her incredible help in editing and making sense of my writing.

Thank you, Paul Doherty for always helping me see the brighter picture and Robert Henderson for being the friend one needs while navigating through such a book.

So many have encouraged and so many have prophesied. I thank each one.

DEDICATION

I would like to dedicate this book to my family who have walked with me all these years but especially to my grandchildren, whom I long to see blessed and walking in the blessing of God. Brandon, Nate, Annalyse and Ariana. Bless you with the blessings of your grandfather.

OTHER BOOKS

BY DENNIS PAUL GOLDSWORTHY-DAVIS

Unlimited Anointings

The God of Jacob

Grace Looks Good on You

Walking in The Prophetic

Standing In the Perfect Storm

TABLE OF CONTENTS

FOREWORD

When we speak of or talk about being blessed, it means there is a supernatural essence that is touching our lives. This essence will cause us to overcome any and all adversity to live a life of success and significance. It doesn't mean that we will be without challenges or even struggles. David spoke of this in Psalms 124:1-8 when he declared what would have happened had God not been for them.

Psalm 124:1–8 (NKJV)
1 "If it had not been the Lord who was on our side,"
Let Israel now say—
2 "If it had not been the Lord who was on our side,
When men rose up against us,
3 Then they would have swallowed us alive,
When their wrath was kindled against us;
4 Then the waters would have overwhelmed us,
The stream would have gone over our soul;
5 Then the swollen waters
Would have gone over our soul."
6 Blessed be the Lord,
Who has not given us as prey to their teeth.
7 Our soul has escaped as a bird from the snare of the fowlers;
The snare is broken, and we have escaped.
8 Our help is in the name of the Lord,
Who made heaven and earth.

Sometimes we think that living a blessed life means no enemies or pains. A blessed life, sometimes means that what comes against us doesn't overwhelm us. We get through it and are left standing when others didn't make it. We weren't swallowed up. We weren't overwhelmed. The floods released against us didn't carry us away. We in fact escaped and what tried to destroy us was broken. I love Psalms 37:35-37.

Psalm 37:35–37 (NKJV)
35 I have seen the wicked in great power,
And spreading himself like a native green tree.
36 Yet he passed away, and behold, he was no more;
Indeed I sought him, but he could not be found.
37 Mark the blameless man, and observe the upright;
For the future of that man is peace.

The wicked seem to spread out and enlarge themselves. They, for a season have great success and prowess. Yet we are told he passes away and is no more. The blameless man however has a future. The King James Version says, "the end of that man is peace. Sometimes we evaluate too soon whether someone or even we ourselves are blessed. We should allow the procedures of God to work. I Corinthians 4:5 tells us not to be too quick to call something cursed of God or even blessed of God. Time will reveal and tell who the hand of God is really on.

1 Corinthians 4:5 (NKJV)
5 Therefore judge nothing before the time, until the Lord comes, who will both bring to light the hidden things of darkness and reveal the counsels of the hearts. Then each one's praise will come from God.

The Lord will unveil where the true blessings of God really rest.

With this being said, we must desire the commanded blessing of God. It is this blessing that leads to success, significance and strength to fulfill the agendas that God has assigned us. In this book, "Gaining The Commanded Blessings", my friend Dennis Goldsworthy-Davis unlocks secrets to this little known and discussed principle. From his prophetic mantle, he shares ideas and concepts to embracing this principle or maybe better yet, to be embraced by it. When the commanded blessing overtakes our lives, everything changes. Doors open, opportunities are given, favors are shown and even the blessing of God that makes rich and adds no sorrow begins to operate. This is because we have come under the auspices of God's favor. His touch and lovingkindness have now impacted our lives. We are moving into the season we have awaited. It's time to go forward and live out the dreams of previous years. Those years are over. Now we must steward the bounty of what God has trusted us with because of His Commanded Blessing!

Robert Henderson
Best-selling Author of The Court of Heaven Series

INTRODUCTION

Many years ago I heard a preacher make a statement that has never left me. He had clearly moved into a place of great blessing and success. This was the statement: "I learned to stop asking the Lord to bless what I was doing but rather to ask him to show me what he was blessing." When he was given his answer he jumped into another realm of ministry all together.

There is no doubt that God is a God of blessing! He first blesses in Genesis when he has made man.

> *"God blessed them and said, "Be fruitful and increase in number and fill the water in the seas, and let the birds increase on the earth."*
> Genesis 1:22

His intention was that man would walk in his blessing. He also speaks blessing in Revelation, once again aimed at man.

> *"Blessed are those who wash their robes, that they may have the right to the tree of life and may go through the gates into the city."* Revelation 22:14

The Lord starts in creation and the first Chapter of the Bible, with blessing man and then in the last Chapter of revelation, reveals his heart to bless man. In other words, MAN WAS CREATED TO BE BLESSED AND TO WALK IN HIS BLESSING! God has made his intention known, written it and then desires that man walk in it. All we have to do is find what it is that he blesses.

The commanded blessing is very simply the place where the Lord has preordained he will bless. He has preset that blessing, spoken about it and often (like in the life of Abraham) given men the way into it. What is great about this is that Abraham was not alone in his blessing. In fact, we read in Galatians that we can be blessed alongside Abraham!

> *"So those who rely on faith are blessed along with Abraham, the man of faith."* Galatians 3:9

Speaking of such a place of blessing, these words are actually recorded by the psalmist. The KJV says it in a beautiful way:

> *"For there the Lord commanded the blessing."* Psalm 133:3 KJV

It's a done deal! What revelation the psalmist had: There are places that the blessing has been preordained in the heart of the one who created us to be blessed by the creator! What is great about our God is that he reveals these places both in the word and prophetically when he speaks to man, as he did to Abraham in Genesis 12. We can search it out in his Logos word, have it revealed by the Spirit of God himself or find others walking in such blessing and learn from their revelations and life lessons.

What a journey we are about to take in this book as we search out how to gain the places of commanded blessing.

CHAPTER ONE
THE FIRST COMMANDED BLESSING

The first commanded blessing is found three times in the book of Genesis. They are all the same blessing, it is the blessing on his created man!

> *"He blessed them and said..."*
> Genesis 1:22, 1:28 and 5:2

What was this first commanded blessing? It was threefold:

> Firstly, they were blessed in the image of God so the blessing of being the representation of God.
>
> > *"Then God said, 'Let us make mankind in our image, in our likeness, so that they may rule over the fish in the seas and the birds in the sky....' "* Genesis 1:26
>
> Secondly, blessed in his likeness with the ability to carry the divine and to act on his behalf!
>
> Thirdly, so that we could rule and have dominion. What a blessing humankind has been given! And clearly it is still functional today.

Now comes the fourth blessing, another threefold blessing:

> *"Be fruitful and increase...fill the earth and subdue it. Rule over...every living creature."* Genesis1:28.

Firstly, the ability to be fruit. In what way? They were blessed to be fruitful in the womb, fruitful in labor and fruitful in whatever the hand turns to.

Secondly, the ability to increase. They were blessed to become greater in number and in all ways. Nothing static in this promise!

Thirdly, the ability to fill the earth and subdue. Here is the blessing of the earth being given to us as an inheritance and that the earth would become subject to us and everything in it.

So great was this blessing that the enemy of both God and humankind wanted to come and steal it by trickery! The thief mentioned by Jesus arrived to steal the blessing given to humankind.

> *"The thief comes only to steal and kill and destroy..."* John 10:10

This manifests so clearly in Genesis. Previously it was mentioned that in Genesis 1:28 God blessed them. The enemy came to steal the blessing by challenging with these words:

> *"Did God really say...?"* Genesis 3:1

Or as the KJV says,

> *"Hath God said..."* Genesis 3:1 KJV

He challenges his promise, he challenges his blessing, and he challenges his command, as though he is saying, "Come on, throw that blessing away, give it to me, you don't need it." Sure enough, the rouse worked. Humankind threw away some of his God given blessing BUT thankfully to be later redeemed by the Last Adam, Christ himself!

> *"So it is written: "The first man Adam became a living being", the last Adam, a life-giving spirit."*
> 1 Corinthians 15:45

Now that is who our Blesser is! He intended us to be blessed so sent another Adam to redeem all that was lost. And redeem it he did. We will see his blessings manifest soon enough!

CHAPTER 2
THE BEGINNING OF ABRAHAM'S BLESSING
"I will bless you"

Abraham, who opens the door of personal blessing and relationship with God to us all, springs into our sight in Genesis 12. At this time his name has not been changed. He is still called Abram. More will be said of this name change later.

This door Abraham opens is the door into the place where God says,

> *"I will make you into a great nation, and I will bless you..."* Genesis 12:2

Now the very statement, "I will", means it is predetermined but must clearly be walked into. I believe our Lord has a huge "I will bless" for us all. Like Abraham, we must learn to walk into it.

Let's look at the rest of God's statement to Abraham and at the promise of blessing found in Genesis.

> *"...will bless you; I will make your name great, and you will be a blessing. I will bless those who bless you, and whoever curses you I will curse; and all peoples on earth will be blessed through you."* Genesis 12:2 (continued) -3

Stated again, God is saying:

> I will make you into a great nation
> I will bless you
> I will make your name great
> You will be a blessing
> I will bless those, who bless you
> Whoever curses you I will curse
> All the people of the earth will be blessed through you.

Now that is one great promise of blessing! It is important to anyone studying the commanded blessing because, as mentioned in the introduction, we are promised in

Galatians just like Abraham was promised that we can be blessed alongside or with him in the same manner.

> *"So those who rely on faith are blessed along with Abraham, the man of faith."* Galatians 3:9

In summary of the statement, "I will bless", we see a sevenfold promise. This was a blessing that went far beyond himself but surely that is what blessing really is. It cannot be contained. I believe later in the Bible when Jabez asks for blessing he is asking for the same measure of blessing.

> *"Jabez cried out to the God of Israel, 'Oh, that thou wouldest bless me indeed..."*
> 1 Chronicles 4:10 KJV

In the original language it says, "Oh that you would bless me, bless me." I want to be a blessing! Interesting, too, that the Lord granted his request. There again we see God's desire to bless!

What was the determining factor for receiving God's statement, "I will bless"? Here it is!

> *"The Lord had said to Abram, "Go from your country, your people and your father's household to the land I will show you."* Genesis 12:1

He was to leave his past and his reliance on his family and venture out with God. God's command to "Go to the land I will show you", required of Abram a trust factor, a faith and a reliance that God would do what he said he would do. This would be a pilgrimage that would have no guarantee but that God would do what he said he would do! Gosh, how this is like salvation when we put our trust in the Christ and begin to follow, leaving all behind. The word speaks of this:

> *"Blessed are those whose strength is in you, whose hearts are set on pilgrimage."* Psalm 84:5

Leaving our past, is more than just a reliance issue. It often involves letting go of anything that would stop the blessing of God being able to fully function in our lives. It is actually the act of giving the Lord the full ability to be God in our lives. We become fully reliant on his word and life. We leave in our weakness and let him release his strength in us!

> *"So Abram went, as the Lord told him."*
> Genesis 12:4

The journey through that door into God's promise, "I will bless", had begun.

CHAPTER 3
BLESSINGS INITIATED AND RELEASED

The offer, "I will bless you" of our last chapter finds itself suddenly starting to be initiated in Genesis 14.

> *"And he blessed Abram, saying, "Blessed be Abram by God most high."* Genesis 14:19

The key to the initiation is paramount not only to Abraham but also to us for today. The key was who initiated the blessing and what he did when he did it. The initiator was none other than Melchizedek, the king of Salem. The book of Hebrews shares this about him:

> *"...king of Salem and priest of God Most High... First, the name...means 'king of righteousness'', then also, 'king of Salem' means 'king of peace."*
> Hebrews 7:1-2

Guess who Abraham met! Guess who initiated the blessing of God! This was none other than Jesus before he came as the son of man. Melchizedek meets Abraham, brings out the bread and wine and blesses him. Through the blood and body of Christ the blessings of God are released to the Christian. When we participate in his death we get his life and it opens to us the blessings of the sons of God!

We watch this scenario with deep interest and loving hearts!

> Melchizedek initiates the encounter
> Melchizedek brings the bread and wine
> Melchizedek releases the Blessing
> Abraham recognizes who he is and tithes to him.

Jesus said,

> *"No one can come to me unless the father who sent me draws them."* John 6:44

Initiated of God! He offers that we participate in his death and resurrection. He then releases his blessing. As we receive him and his blessing like Abraham, our father in faith, we tithe to him who is living and we are blessed that have the promises of blessing!

> *"This man, however, did not trace his descent from Levi, yet he collected a tenth from Abraham and blessed him who had the promises. And without doubt the lesser is blessed by the greater. In the one case, the tenth is collected by people who die; but in the other case, by him who is declared to be living."* Hebrews 7:6-8

So, Jesus is the key to the blessings of God being released! But our response to live a life dedicated to the Lord causes the blessings to be not only initiated but spoken over our lives. He who gained the fullness from the father shares his blessings with us.

There it is! The commanded blessing.

CHAPTER 4
THE BLESSING LIVED OUT

So, what did the blessing of Abraham look like? Here are just some of his blessings:

> He was blessed to have friendship with God. This within itself brings relationship and promises and encounters.
>
> > *"But you, Israel, my servant, Jacob, whom I have chosen, you descendants of Abraham my friend..."* Isaiah 41:8.
>
> He was blessed among people. Abraham is recognized as a prince among people.
>
> > *"...You are a mighty prince among us."* Genesis 23:6

He was blessed to received non-stop personal promises from Genesis 12 through to Genesis 22.

> He was blessed to be a man of great wealth:
>
> > *"Abram had become very wealthy in livestock and in silver and gold."* Genesis 13:2

He was blessed to have his name God changed to what God saw him to be:

> *"...your name will be Abraham, for I have made you a father of many nations."* Genesis 17:5

He was blessed to have his body personally revolutionized to become a Father in old age.

He was blessed to have his children follow him.

> *"For I have chosen him, so that he will direct his children and his household after him to keep the way of the Lord...."* Genesis 18:19

He was blessed to be man who found favor with God.

> *"If I have found favor in your eyes, my lord, do not pass your servant by."* Genesis 18:3

He was blessed to be a man of great descendants.

> *"...Look up at the sky and count the stars.... So shall your offspring be."* Genesis 15:5

He was blessed to be a man given faith by God.

> *"Abram believed the lord..."* Genesis 15: 5-6

He was blessed to be a man who was a blessing to others.

> *"...I will make your name great and you will be a blessing."* Genesis 12:2

The list could go on and on, but we can see some of what blessings can look like. I kept one juicy morsel slightly separate to the others. Why? Because it carries such a promise.

> *"That in blessing I will bless thee, and in multiplying I will multiply thy seed as the stars of the heaven, and as the sand which is upon the sea shore; and thy seed shall possess the gate of his enemies..."* Genesis 22:17 KJV

Beat that for a blessing. Double fold blessing. Blessing within blessing. One man opened the door to generations of blessed victorious people. He must be speaking not just naturally but to the coming of the church.

Remember, we are blessed alongside him. These blessings and so many more are offered to us, too!

CHAPTER 5
MISUNDERSTOOD PROMISES

When you are so blessed by God who wouldn't think that whatever venture you move into would just be blessed by God because of you? But this book is about the commanded blessing not the presumed blessing!

Listen to this statement made by Abraham himself:

"...If only Ishmael might live under your blessing!"
Genesis 17:18.

Whaaaat? Here is God telling him of the blessing he is about to release in his life and he cries out, "No! Bless what I have done. Bless my actions. Bless my interpretation of your promise.". Friend, what a lesson! God commands blessing that is initiated from him, not from us. So many have fallen prey to this. We ourselves live in a time when we wish Abraham would never have tried to help God out in such a way. Ishmael is exemplary of mans' producing for himself what was never promised, and at what results. How can this have ever happened?

It happens when we feel that we are so blessed that whatever we do will be blessed. Not so!

It happens when we try to help God out because he is not walking according to our timetable.

It happens whenever others interpret what the Lord actually told you. This was, sadly, what happened with his wife Sarah but Abraham allowed it as did Adam in the garden of Eden.

It happens when we try to please man rather than God. Paul speaks of this.

"If I were still trying to please people, I would not be a servant of Christ."
Galatians 1:10

It happens when something looks like God in the flesh.

It happens when we try in the flesh to fulfill what can only be done by the Spirit. Paul warns,

> *"Are you so foolish? After beginning by means of the Spirit, are you now trying to finish by means of the flesh?"* Galatians 3:3

The results of trying to initiate our own blessing can touch and affect our lives and the lives of many.

Perhaps we should pray like Jabez, "Oh that you would bless me, bless me.". The word for *bless* here is *Barak*, the word we use to bless God. Here is what the prayer means: *Bless me in a way that will bring blessing to you.*

Never presume when it comes to blessing but listen closely to the commands.

CHAPTER 6
THE BLESSINGS INHERITED

As we have clearly seen in previous chapters, the inheritance of Abraham's blessing was that his descendants would be blessed. This would pass down all the way to us as promised in Galatians 3. But to watch its commencement with both Isaac and Jacob is a great lesson. For instance, the Lord appears two times to Isaac in Genesis 26 and mentions Abraham both times. In verse 3 and verse 24 he is promising to bless the son. Clearly this was built on what he promised Abraham but now offering the son the same inheritance. We are called to be the sons of God according to Galatians 4 and Romans 8:14-17. With that call is the offered inheritance gained by Jesus. With both Isaac and Jacob, Abraham gained the blessing but the sons inherited it, yet always with the same offer as to Abraham: "If you will…, I will…"!

Watch how the Lord visits Jacob:

> *"I am the Lord, the God of your father Abraham and the God of Isaac."* Genesis 28:13

Abraham opened the door. Now the grandson has the opportunity to walk into the blessing. He surely does as we will observe in later chapters.

We see the power of the blessed one to pass on the blessing in Genesis 27 and the first verse of Genesis 28. This is the son who stepped into his father's blessing and is now passing on that blessing. This is the son of whom, after being visited by his father's God, the Bible says,

> *"Isaac reopened the wells that had been dug in the time of his father Abraham, which the Philistines had stopped up after Abraham died, and he gave them the same names his father had given them."* Genesis 26:18

He stepped into his father's blessing. Then if we read on in this chapter we see he stepped into his own blessing and then passed it to his sons. He particularly passed this blessing to his son Jacob.

Inherited blessing is part of the commanded blessing! What was gained by Abraham was accessible for his sons. What an example they were in the way they fought for their inheritance. We have this blessing as sons of Abraham but more so as sons of God and co-heirs with Jesus.

> *"Now if we are children, then we are heirs—heirs of God and co-heirs with Christ, if indeed we share in his sufferings in order that we may also share in his glory."* Romans 8:17.

Equally what has been gained can in turn be imparted. Both Isaac and Jacob do this with their gained blessing. Look at Jacob as he blesses Joseph.

> *"Then he blessed Joseph and said, 'May the God before whom my fathers Abraham and Isaac walked faithfully, the God who has been my shepherd all my life to this day, the Angel who has delivered me from all harm—may he bless these boys...'..."*
> Genesis 48:15-16

Then look again as he blesses all his sons in Genesis 49! It makes you so excited to gain and impart what God has commanded we are to have. Now through us the one who said, "Let us make man in our image.", and who preordained blessing can continue his commanded blessing.

CHAPTER 7

NOT LETTING GO

As we have been looking at the commanded blessing of God we realize more, and yet more, that we are involved in gaining that blessing. Often we are involved by obedience and often by sacrifice but we also need one thing that two people show us so wonderfully. We need the desire that drives us to have what is promised us. Both Jacob and Jabez show this desire so powerfully.

In Genesis 25 and the whole of Genesis 27 we observe Jacob, the one who grabbed his brother's heel as they were born. He clearly knew even in the womb what was his destiny and began to wrestle for it. He wrestled with his brother for the blessing that belonged to the firstborn but would later have an opportunity to wrestle again for the blessing that only God could give. This is the one who at great physical cost makes this statement:

> *"I will not let you go unless you bless me."*
> Genesis 32:26

WHAT A STATEMENT OF INTENT! "I WILL NOT LET YOU GO UNTIL..." I know what is mine, I know what is promised, I know my inheritance and I want it! I want it!

Such was his desire that the Lord himself came from heaven physically to impart it to him. Such was his desire that his name was changed and he became Israel. He became the one who as a prince prevailed with the Lord.

> *"Then the man said, 'Your name will no longer be Jacob, but Israel, because you have struggled with God and with humans and have overcome.'."* Genesis 32:28

So powerful was his intent that he wrestled God and had a face to face encounter!

> *"So Jacob called the place Peniel, saying 'It is because I saw God face to face, and yet my life was spared.'."* Genesis 32:30

We could write chapters on this subject and in fact in another book, *Touching the God of Jacob*, it is dealt with far more intensely. Surely if Jacob can do it, we can do it?? That's why he is called the God of Jacob over fifteen times just in the Psalms. By his statements we see David clearly touched God the same way:

> *"Such is the generation of those who seek him, who seek your face, God of Jacob."* Psalm 24:6

Now let's look at a far more obscure character, the man named Jabez. So obscure is he that only several verses of the Bible are dedicated to him but wow do they reveal something quite spectacular.

> *"Jabez was more honorable than his brothers. His mother had named him Jabez, saying, 'I gave birth to him in pain.'. Jabez cried out to the God of Israel, 'Oh, that you would bless me and enlarge my territory! Let your hand be with me, and keep me from harm so that I will be free from pain.' And God granted his request."* 1 Chronicles 4: 9-10

He is named Jabez as a curse from his mother. The name's meaning, *pain and trouble and grief,* became fulfilled in his life and he suffered pain as the name said he would. Just like Jacob, Jabez became convinced that the blessing that belonged to Abraham could be his. He sought the Lord and asked for this blessing. His prayer asks the God of Abraham to bless him. Verse 10 in the King James Translation reads,

> *"And Jabez called on the God of Israel, saying, Oh that thou wouldest bless me indeed...."*
> 1 Chronicles 4:10 KJV

The word *indeed*, as mentioned before, was actually a repeat of the word *bless*. To be blessed to be a blessing! Sound familiar? Enlarged borders to be a blessing! The hand of God with me to be a blessing! "AND GOD

Granted his request." Yes, there it is again. Like Jacob, Jabez gained the blessing of God despite his circumstances.

These two examples are just that: two of many examples of those that pressed into the commanded blessing. Friends, we are here to gain that which the Almighty desires to give us. WE TOO, WILL NOT LET YOU GO UNTIL YOU BLESS US ALSO!

CHAPTER 8
THE MOUNT GERIZIM BLESSINGS

When the nation of Israel was to enter the promised land two mountains were separated for them to pronounce both curses and blessings. Gerizim was designated for blessings and Ebal for curses.

> *"When you have crossed the Jordan, these tribes shall stand on Mount Gerizim to bless the people...and these tribes shall stand on Mount Ebal to pronounce curses..."* Deuteronomy 27:12-13.

The Gerizim blessings are found in Deuteronomy 28:1-14. And what blessings they were, but they came with a premise! What was that? It was the premise of fully obeying and of not following other Gods.

> *"If you fully obey the Lord your god and carefully follow all his commands I give you today, the lord*

> *your god will set you high above all the nations on earth.*" Deuteronomy 28:1

> *"Do not turn aside from any of the commands I give you today, to the right or to the left, following other gods and serving them."* Deuteronomy 28:14

There is a commanded blessing given for those who set their hearts to follow God and allow his Spirit to direct them. The Lord later speaks of his servant, Caleb:

> *"But because my servant Caleb has a different spirit and follows me wholeheartedly, I will bring him into the land he went to, and his descendants will inherit it."* Numbers 14:24

Caleb's obedience gets the promises for him and his descendants, too. Now listen to the word given to Joshua:

> *"...Be careful to obey all the law my servant Moses gave you; do not turn from it to the right or left, that you may be successful wherever you go.... Then you will be prosperous and successful."* Joshua 1:7,8

Both Joshua and Caleb walked into the land of Israel and gained great success due to their spirit of obedience.

What this commanded blessing demands is a different spirited people. We saw that The Lord spoke of this when he blessed Caleb in Numbers 14:24. David cried out for such a spirit:

> *"Create in me a pure heart, O god, and renew a steadfast spirit within me. Do not cast me from your presence or take your Holy Spirit from me. Restore to me the joy of your salvation and grant me a willing spirit, to sustain me."* Psalm 51:10-12

Here he cries for a right spirit, for the Spirit of the Lord to be upon him and for a spirit of nobility. This, my friends, is all offered to us in Romans 8 when we receive the Spirit of Christ. The whole chapter shows us how the Holy Spirit helps us become the sons of God who inherit.

Let's quickly look at the Gerizim blessings of Deuteronomy 28 and note *All these blessings will come,* not one or two:

Blessed wherever you are in Verse 3
Blessed with children and possessions in Verse 4
Blessed in work in Verse 5
Blessed in travel in Verse 6
Blessed against your enemies in Verse 7
Blessed in everything you do in Verse 8
He will establish you in Verse 9
He will make you his people in Verse 9
He will call you by his name in Verse 10
Abundance of prosperity in Verse 11
Bless the work of your hands in Verse12
Open his storehouse of bounty in Verse12
You will become the lender not the borrower in Verse 12
You will be the head and not the tail in Verse 13.

Wow, one cries, wow! That sounds like a summary of all blessings to me. These are the Lord's intentions for those who allow his Spirit to change them and become different spirited.

CHAPTER 9
THE BLESSINGS OF THE LOVERS OF THE WORD OF GOD

I for one love the Psalms intensely. They are full of revelation and experience and relationship with God. Written mainly by perhaps one of the greatest lovers of God that ever lived. How fitting that the first Psalm has recorded the commanded blessings. This psalm makes a clear line definition of the blessings that belong to the lovers of the word of God!

Psalm 1 shows us that life is a choice. We can live by and love the word of God or hang around with the crowd that scoffs and lives for itself. We can choose the word of God or the *"counsel of the ungodly"* as KJV so aptly says in verse 1. We can choose to stand on the word or stand in the way of the wicked. Will we sit in heavenly places with Christ (Ephesians 2:6) or in the seat of the mockers. One reigns with Christ, the other sits in judgment on other people. Clear line choices and with clear line results.

The ungodly or wicked by choice are like chaff the wind blows away (Verse 4). No stability there! No future and no

blessing. They will not stand when God judges (Verse 5) and will not be found in the congregation of the righteous. They won't be found among the worshippers or in the bride of Christ. They made their choice.
The blessings on the lovers of the word are beautiful indeed. They delight in the word. They love it! It is their joy and entertainment! They like to read it and hear it and follow it and meditate on it. It becomes their lifestyle. To make it plain and simple, they have learned this:

> *"Man does not live on bread alone but on every word that comes from the mouth of the Lord."*
> Deuteronomy 8:3

If you want to know what this looks like, read Psalm 119. What a psalm of a word-lover that is!

So, let's look at the commanded blessings in Psalm 1:

> Blessed to be like a tree planted in Verse 3. Unmovable…if you follow the plantings of the Lord both in Psalm 92:12 and Isaiah 61:3 this blessing is huge.
>
> Blessed to be fruit bearers for God in the seasons of God in Verse 3. His fruit from a life of word-living!
>
> Whose leaf does not wither in Verse 3. No drought here and no being burned out but a continued life of blessing.

Blessed to prosper in whatever they do in Verse 3. Now that is a WOW, to prosper in every arena of life. Much like the promises of Deuteronomy 28 from the last chapter.

Blessed to stand in the assembly of the righteous in Verse 5. You are never alone but part of a larger family of God. God gives you a support group. You find yourself in worship continually and in the congregation of the ones who praise! You are drawn by God into fellowship with himself and his people.

Blessed to be named righteous in Verses 5 and 6. Being justified with God. Being affected not just by the *Logos* of God, *his written word*, but by the Word himself, the Christ. It is worth mentioning my friend, Alan Vincent, here. As he studied the word of God to find an answer to what someone with wrong doctrine was saying he found the word himself and was born again. He became one of the most prolific teachers and apostolic men of my generation!

Blessed to be watched over by him. What a blessing! One of my favorite psalms covers this deeply, Psalm 121. It explains what happens when God watches over you. It is basically that he watches over you day and night, shades you and travels with you. I personally have lived by this for years. It is reinforced in Psalm 121. This is an eternal promise my friends, not a momentary one.

> *"the Lord will watch over your coming and going both now and forevermore."* Psalm 121:8

Every commanded blessing is deeply intriguing and intense but one cannot help but be affected by the depth of promise given in this small psalm. It is the first mentioned psalm which means one should please note carefully what is written.

CHAPTER 10
FRIENDSHIP WITH GOD

Job, while lamenting his former days makes a massive statement,

> *"Oh, for the days when I was in my prime, when God's intimate friendship blessed my house."* Job 29:4

This is translated the same in the ASV and other versions. In the NKJV it is translated,

> *"...the friendly counsel of God was over my tent."* Job 29:4 NKJV

Quite simply, this is the blessing that comes from relationship and friendship with God. Why is it a commanded blessing? Because it comes with him. You get him. You get his blessing!

Can a man be a friend of God? Well, let's look and see. God himself calls Abraham his friend.

> *"...you descendants of Abraham my friend..."*
> Isaiah 41:8

Let's be honest. We have already looked at the blessings of Abraham. So if, according to Galatians 3, we can be blessed alongside Abraham that means we can also have friendship with God. Now let's look at what Jesus says to his disciples:

> *"I no longer call you servants, because a servant does not know his master's business. Instead, I have called you friends, for everything that I learned from my Father I have made known to you."*
> John 15:15

Jesus makes it clear that his servants can become his friends but with the blessing of personal revelation. Servants don't get the personal touch that friends do. They don't share in the intimate secrets from the lips of our Lord. Friendship is also intimated with the word *fellowship*, which is the Greek word *koinonia.* We are told in various New Testament passages that we have this option in our Christian walk. In fact, we are told that part of our call was into the fellowship of Jesus.

> *"God is faithful, who has called you into fellowship with his Son, Jesus Christ our Lord."*
> 1 Corinthians 1:9

This is an awesome truth available to all! Twice in the New Testament fellowship is used regarding the Holy Spirit.

> *"May the grace of the Lord Jesus Christ, and the love of God, and the fellowship of the Holy Spirit be with you all."* 2 Corinthians 13:14

> *"Therefore if you have any.... common sharing in the Spirit,..."* Philippians 2:1

The latter speaks like this is the KJV: "If there be any fellowship". This means we can fellowship, but will we? So, friendship is not only possible but is deeply encouraged.

What are the blessings that come from fellowship? Abraham's blessings to start with. Job says this relationship blessed his whole household and we know of his vast blessings. The disciples had intimate things shared. We could go on but my favorite blessing to share is this:

> *"The Lord would speak with Moses face to face, as one speaks to a friend."* Exodus 33:11

Now there is a blessing indeed! We study the face of God with Moses, who shone with glory according to Exodus 34:29-30. Jacob saw God face to face and received the blessing, a new name and the promise of the blessing falling on his family. The blessings that come with friendship with God are so numerous that no one chapter could cover them but surely worth a deep search. To be a friend of God would bring everything that his presence and person could bring. Let's become desirous of such a relationship. The evidence would become quite obvious.

CHAPTER 11
THE BLESSING OF RELIANCE ON GOD

One of my favorite psalms is Psalm 84. The reason is that it covers the journey of those who come to put their trust and life in God.

> *"Blessed are those whose strength is in you, whose hearts are set on pilgrimage."* Psalm 84:5

The same heart is reflected in the words of this old worship song:

> *"My life is in you Lord, my strength and my hope are in you."* by Daniel Gardner

To make God my strength means I have made God my refuge and put my trust in him. Self-reliance just went out the window. Paul speaks of a place where he found out that self-reliance doesn't work.

> *"...about the troubles we experienced... We were under great pressure, far beyond our ability to endure...felt the sentence of death... But this*

> *happened that we might not rely on ourselves but on God, who raises the dead."* 2 Corinthians 1:8-9

He found that relying on God brought a deliverance to him in great trials. Later in the same book Paul says that relying on God's strength released tremendous grace in his life.

> *"But he said to me, 'My grace is sufficient for you, for my power is made perfect in weakness.' ...That is why, for Christ's sake, I delight in weaknesses.... For when I am weak, then I am strong."*
> 2 Corinthians 12:9-10.

Let's look at what relying on God's strength could look like:

> Relying on his Holy Spirit to strengthen our inner man. Who doesn't need that? Ephesians 3:16
>
> Relying on his grace in every situation
> 2 Corinthians 12:9
> Receiving his anointing, as the strength in the passage is that of the Greek word *dunamis* which is *the anointing power of God.* 2 Corinthians
>
> Receiving his deliverance in times of need.
> 2 Corinthians 1:10
>
> All that comes from God including the help of men and angels. Hebrews 1:14 and 2 Corinthians 1.

Receiving encouragement. One version of scripture says,

"David found strength in his God."
1 Samuel 30:6

Whereas another version says,

"he encouraged himself in the Lord God." 1 Samuel 30:6 KJV

Which is right? Both are. When the Lord encourages us, he strengthens us and when he strengthens he encourages.

The actual power of God touching and filling and blessing. Paul speaks of it as,

"the working of his mighty power."
Ephesians 1:19

Later in Ephesians we're told he is,

"... able to do exceedingly abundantly above all that we ask or think, according to the power that worketh in us."
Ephesians 3: 20 KJV.

There are no limits when we rely on his strength and power and the blessings!

Within the passage in Psalm 84, some of the blessings are enumerated:

His journey is released within us in verse 5.

He enables us to see the life of God in the middle of difficult times thus blessing others with our overflow in verse 6 (beautiful verse).

Strength increases. When you make God your strength, he increases that strength again and again! Verse 7

Then there is the clear face to face with the Lord in verse 7.

But the psalm goes on with other blessings!

He becomes the God of Jacob to us which is filled with its own promises in Verse 8,

He releases favor in Verse 9,

He gives protection in Verse 10,

He gives favor and honor and the promise of all the blessings combined in Verse 11,

> *"NO GOOD THING WILL HE WITHHOLD."* Psalm 84:11 KJV emphasis added

Nothing held back! Gosh, talk about the commanded blessing!

The psalmist finishes this great psalm with all its promises with this:

> *"Lord Almighty, blessed is the one who trusts in you."* Psalm 84:12

For the third time the word *blessed* is used. Talk about the Lord wanting us to catch his intent! Three times he uses the word *blessed*. Three times means that it is established in God.

It's time to read and digest and to make a decision that the Lord is going to be my strength, but one could not write of such a truth without the famous passage in Isaiah being mentioned and implied:

> *"But those who wait on"* (entangle themselves with) *"the Lord shall renew their strength, they shall mount up with wings like eagles, they shall run and not be weary, they shall walk and not faint."* Isaiah 40:31 NKJV

We choose to rely on him and then we throw ourselves on him and entangle ourselves with him, expecting nothing less than his promises to be fulfilled. I know for me this has been true again and again!

CHAPTER 12
BLESSED IS THE MAN THAT FEARS THE LORD

Two separate Psalms have the commanded blessing concerning the fear of the Lord:

> *"Blessed are all who fear the Lord, who walk in obedience to him."* Psalms 128:1

> *"Blessed are those who fear the Lord, who find great delight in his commands."* Psalms 112:1

Before we can examine the commanded blessing we must ascertain what *the fear of the Lord* means. Is it dread? Is it terror? Those words are associated with fear and can be found in the Old Testament more than once. For the believer and Godly the fear of the Lord is different! It simply means *reverent and standing in awe*. In fact, those words are actually used dependent on the translation.

> *"Let all the inhabitants of the world stand in awe of him."* Psalm 33: 8 KJV

> *"Let all the people of the world revere him."* Psalm 33:8

Really, to *fear* him is *to put him in right prospective in honor and awe*. The commanded blessings for such people are magnanimous.

The fear of the Lord is a choice. To say, "Blessed is the man that fears the Lord", clearly means many don't. But how do you gain such a reverence? Reverence comes by:

> Receiving, longing for and treasuring what the word of God teaches in our lives.

"Accepting my words and storing up my commands within you..." Proverbs 2:1
"Blessed are those who fear the Lord, who find great delight in his commands." Psalms 112:1

Knowing him as he is and having an intimate knowledge of God. Proverbs 2

Learning from those who have it. We must remember most things we have gained are learned. When we meet others who have a fear of the Lord we can gain from their lives such a reverence and walk.
"Come, my children, listen to me; I will teach you the fear of the Lord." Psalms 34:11

Encountering the Holy Spirit!
"The Spirit of the lord will rest on him--
...the Spirit of the knowledge and fear of the Lord--" Isaiah 11:2.
When we encounter him, either as the *Spirit of Christ* referred to in Romans 8 or the powerful baptizer Jesus spoke of in Acts 1:8, he will come into us as one who carries and imparts the fear of the Lord.

The commanded blessings that come with the fear of the Lord are so numerous that it would take a book to remunerate them. But here are a few:

"The fear of the Lord leads to life; then one rests content, untouched by trouble." Proverbs 19:23

"The angel of the Lord encamps around those that fear him, and he delivers them." Psalms 34:7

"Their children will be mighty in the land" Psalms 112:2

"Wealth and riches are in their houses," Psalms 112:3

"You eat the fruit of your labor," Psalms 128:2

"Your wife will be like a fruitful vine," Psalms 128:3

"Your children will be like olive shoots around your table." Psalms 128:3

"May the Lord bless you from Zion," (his dwelling place) Psalms 128:5

"...may you see the prosperity of Jerusalem..." Psalms 128:5. Seeing the Kingdom of God prosper in your lifetime!

"May you live to see your children's children—" Psalms 128:6. That means living a long life.

No wonder it is said,

"The fear of the Lord is the beginning of wisdom." Psalm 111:10

It unlocks many blessings from God. Let's set our heart to fear him my friends!

CHAPTER 13

THE BLESSING OF UNITY

Psalm 133 is a small enough psalm but packed with truth and suddenly in verse 3, we read,

> *"For there the Lord commands the blessing."*
> Psalm 133:3

What causes this command? The word *for* makes you look carefully at the previous verses:

> The first Verse speaks of dwelling together in unity.
>
> The second verse speaks of the anointing oil on the head and then the maturity of the beard and the priesthood.
>
> The third verse speaks of the dew of Hermon and Mount Zion.

What brings the blessing? All of it! He blesses unity, he blesses maturity, he blesses anointing and he blesses his priesthood and the dew. The dew is the representation of his outpouring being seen in Hermon, known as the glistening mountain. He blesses his dwelling place, Mount Zion. It all commands his blessing!

In this chapter let us center on unity because it is the key to such a command:

> *"Behold, how good and how pleasant it is for brethren to dwell together in unity!"*
> Psalm 133:1KJV

Why is unity so important? Because it becomes like the Godhead.

> *"Let us make man in our image, after our likeness."*
> Genesis 1:26 KJV

The Godhead is where everything flows from. Paul speaks of life coming from the head. If we can become like the head, we get the life of the head.

> *"...the head, from whom the whole body, supported and held together by its ligaments and sinews, grows as God causes it to grow."* Colossians 2:19

The Godhead clearly made decisions from unity. *Let us.*

> *"Then God said, 'Let us make mankind in our image'..."* Genesis 1:26

All life from creation came from unity. All life has continued to pour out from unity. Jesus speaks of his oneness with the Father and prays that the church will become one with them. His prayer is that the unity of his relationship with the father, would become the church's relationship too.

> *"...that all of them may be one, Father just as you are in me and I am in you.....I have given them the glory that you gave me, that they may be one as we are one--I in them and you in me—so that they may be brought to complete unity."* John 17:21-23

So, the key to the life Jesus manifested was that of his oneness with the father and the key to the life the early church manifested was their oneness with Jesus and each other.

You cannot break the power on unity! You cannot stop the blessing on unity. But how do we get it? Let's examine:

> Being united with Christ is the beginning. John 17 clearly states when we become one with the unifier himself, Christ, he brings his Spirit of unity into us.
>
> Jesus is praying for unity as we quoted in John 17. The prayer of Jesus is pressing us by the Spirit of God, sent to pray in us.
>
> > *"...but the Spirit himself intercedes for us through wordless groans."* Romans 8:26
>
> Unity comes when touched by the glory in John 17:22. The glory, the Kingdom glory! The weighty presence of God coming not only on us but in us.

It is hard to dwell in the glory of God and become disunited!

Unity comes when we become sanctified by his truth.

> *"Sanctify them by the truth, your word is truth."* John 17:17

Wow, now that changes the word of God from reading material to the truth that sanctifies us. It separates us from the past and self and then separates us to God himself and allows him to show himself in us. What a prayer, Jesus! Let it be so that we become one with you and each other.

We live together in Unity. We saw this statement in Psalm 133:1. It is clear we are to choose to become one with him and then choose to live in unity with each other. We dwell. We don't separate. We break that power of the spirit of divorce in the western world. We choose to dwell and then the blessing is poured out!

The day of Pentecost clearly proves that unity releases the blessing of anointing that glistens from Hermon. Listen to these words:

> *"When the day of Pentecost came, they were all together in one place."* Acts 2:1
> *"...they were all with one accord in one place."* Acts 2:1 KJV

THEY WERE UNIFIED IN DESIRE AND PURPOSE. Bang, commanded blessing!

When we are unified, we come to maturity! James says when we are mature, we lack nothing. God trusts the mature with blessing. When we are in unity we have a corporate priesthood that God can anoint! When we are in unity we become as the head itself and anointing and blessing come from the head! We are in unity and anointed it glistens and stands out before God and man and, *bang* again, He commands the blessing! This is a mission we must choose to flow in and watch the commanded blessing pour out.

CHAPTER 14
THE BLESSING OF BEING UNITED WITH CHRIST

When we studied the blessings on Abraham we found that the promise of being blessed was released when he met Melchizedek. Hebrews 7 makes it so clear that he was the Christ before he came as Jesus. Matthew, quoting the promise of Psalm 118:26, says,

> *"Blessed is he that comes in the name of the Lord,"*
> Matthew 21:9

This is, of course, Jesus himself the crowds were ecstatically quoting. He who was the blessing of the Lord came to release the blessing of the Lord.

There is a simple truth released in the Bible by Jesus himself:

> *"Freely you have received, freely give."*
> Matthew 10:8

This Jesus, who had received the fullness of the blessing of God, came to release that blessing. How? Clearly that blessing was released by his ministry but more so when he was received into the hearts and lives of people.

> *"...If we have any encouragement from being United to Christ...."* Philippians 2:1

When we become united to the Blessed One we automatically walk into the blessings associated with such a Union.

The blessings of being united with Christ would comprise another book in itself but I wanted to open our hearts to some of it. Clearly, first of all, he came to free us from our sin by becoming the sacrifice for that sin. Hebrews Chapter 10 covers this so well as do so many other scriptures. Romans says this brings a commanded blessing in itself.

> *"Blessed are those whose transgressions are forgiven, whose sins are covered."* Romans 4:7

The blessings are so numerous to this. It means we can stand before God fearlessly. That's why it says,

> *"Let us draw near to God with a sincere heart and with the full assurance that faith brings, having our hearts sprinkled to cleanse us from a guilty conscience and having our bodies washed with pure water."* Hebrews 10:22

The blessing of relationship with the living God and so much more!

Truly being United with Christ then opens the door to all God's blessings that are predetermined and preset. Listen to this:

> *"Praise be to the God and Father of our Lord Jesus Christ, who has blessed us in the heavenly realms with every spiritual blessing in Christ."*
> Ephesians 1:3

Notice the word *every*! That means there are no limits to these blessings. They are already put into our *bank account* on our behalf in heaven, ready to be withdrawn and released. Why *bank account*? because they are being held on our behalf in heavenly places!

Then there is the whole realm of the glory of God. As mentioned in a previous chapter, John 17 is where Jesus prays to the father about the church but Verse 22 is particular to us concerning our blessings.

> *"I have given them the glory that you gave me..."*
> John 17:22

This was actually stated before the outpouring of the Holy Spirit. Jesus had already done it beforehand and now was waiting for his resurrection to release it as in Acts chapter 2. Awesome! It's preset that we should have this same glory! That's why Paul, writing to the Colossians, says this:

> *"...Christ in you the hope of glory."*
> Colossians 1:27

This is our blessing, preset and predetermined by God and obtained by Christ for us!

But I have one more! Romans 8 is a chapter of great delight and revelation. We are told that when we receive Christ, he comes by his Spirit into our lives. From that we are adopted into sonship:

> *"...the Spirit you received brought about your adoption to sonship. And by him we cry, 'Abba, Father'."* Romans 8:15

Just writing this makes me want to fall down and worship! The Spirit then leads us into our inheritance!

> *"Now if we are children, then we are heirs--heirs of God and co-heirs with Christ..."* Romans 8:17

Jesus not only procured our sonship but then shares his inheritance with us. Now we are talking about blessing and commanded blessing at that! How do we find it? The Holy Spirit will lead us to it by revelation and importation!

If only we could walk through the fullness of this commanded blessing but, in reality, the whole of the blessings of God really come through Christ. That's why so many writers in the Bible push us to grow in our knowledge of Christ. He is such a key to the commanded blessings.

CHAPTER 15
THE SERMON ON THE MOUNT

JESUS the blessed one, now wanting to do what had been in the heart of God since creation, sits his disciples down and teaches them how to step into God's commanded blessings. The famous sermon on the Mount in its entirety is quite a revelation. It could be the basis for any Christians to live by but we are just going to take the part where Jesus speaks of being blessed. This is particularly special to me because the first sermon I ever preached was from this particular address of Jesus:

> *"Blessed are the peacemakers, for they will be called the children of God."* Matthew 5:9

Little did I know that this would be part of my ministry and equally should be part of all our lives and ministries.

We will limit our discussion to nine items using Matthew 5 for my reference. These are not the only times Jesus releases a potential commanded blessing.

Blessed to inherit the realm that God walks in and rules in and ministers from. What a promise!

> *"Blessed are the poor in spirit, for theirs is the kingdom of heaven."* Matthew 5:3

What is *poor in spirit*? Humble. Knowing our need. Knowing that without him we have nothing. It makes us hungry and desirous!

Blessed to be comforted.

> *"Blessed are those who mourn, for they will be comforted."* Matthew 5:4

Initially this looks like the Lord is just going to turn up to every funeral but it is deeper. David gives us a great revelation:

> *"The sacrifices of God are a broken spirit: a broken and contrite heart, oh God, thou wilt not despise."* Psalm 51:17 KJV

What does this mean? *Contrite*: *quick to repent, soft hearted, and easy to teach and minister to. Broken spirited*: *no longer haughty but needy of his touch and his grace*. These people will be blessed by the Comforter himself. Paul says he not only received this ministry of comfort but was blessed by it in such a way that he could share it with others in 2 Corinthians 1:3-6.

Blessed to inherit the earth.

> *"Blessed are the meek, for they will inherit the earth."* Matthew 5:5

Meekness: mild and humble. No arrogance and harshness. Have you noticed the trait? One New Testament writer referred to it as being *clothed with humility*. We become inheritors and God can give us rule and dominion. He can trust his possessions with us.

Blessed to be filled.

> *"Blessed are those who hunger and thirst for righteousness for they will be filled."* Matthew 5:6

Interesting, they hunger for not just God but being right with God and the ways of God. We are told to

> *"...seek first his kingdom and his righteousness...".* Matthew 6:33

Basically, they hunger for him and his ways in their lives. Jesus himself said, "Anyone that is thirsty, let him come to me and drink." Let God create a thirst that only he can quench! He will quench it. Exciting I say!

Blessed to be shown mercy.

> *"Blessed are the merciful, for they will be shown mercy."* Matthew 5:7

This is the God of goodness and mercy speaking. There are three things the Lord requires, and one of them is that we love mercy.

"And what does the Lord require of you?
To act justly and to love mercy and to walk
humbly with your God." Micah 6:8

Mercy on ourselves, which is often the hardest, and mercy on others. For then we will walk under the mercy of God. Mercy is the key to the release of the goodness of God! Remember, mercy is not deserved but given out of goodness and compassion.

Blessed to see God

"Blessed are the pure in heart, for they will see God." Matthew 5:8

Really, this speaks of those who have allowed their hearts to be cleansed by the blood of the lamb. David cried for it:

"Create in me a clean heart, O God..."
Psalm 51:10 KJV

A pure heart is not just cleansed but its motives are pure. This requires that we have the Spirt of God at work in our hearts at all times. The blessing is to see God. David had a heart after God and look at what he gained:

"...you will fill me with joy in your presence, with eternal pleasures at your right hand." Psalm 16:11

Purify our hearts Lord!

Blessed to be called the sons of God

"Blessed are the peacemakers, for they will be called children of God." Matthew 5:9

I have had much time to think on this. Who is the great peacemaker? The Lord is. He brings us peace and grants us peace. The Holy Spirt brings peace as a fruit of the Spirit.

> *"But the fruit of the Spirit is love, joy, peace..."* Galatians 5:22

Peacemakers bring peace to themselves in relationship to their walk with God but also impart it others as an overflow. More than that, they are the ones who bring calm in the storms of life and church. The blessing? They are called sons of God! By whom? By God himself! Now that opens the blessings that come with sonship.

Blessed to possess the kingdom of Heaven.

> *"Blessed are those who are persecuted because of righteousness, for theirs is the kingdom of heaven."* Matthew 5:10

This seems like a paradox! Being persecuted is a blessing? No. Persecution comes because you carry the one you love so much that they cannot abide him in you! You convict them because of your life. You are now being treated like him! What is the blessing? Not just the Kingdom is yours but the heavenly realms, where it operates. He gives you dominion in his realm.

Blessed because great is your reward in heaven.

> *"Blessed are you when people insult you, persecute you and falsely say all kinds of evil against you because of me. Rejoice and*

be glad, because great is your reward in heaven..." Matthew 5:11-12

Gosh, we live in this day. You can say anything but his name. The verse says, *"rejoice and be glad"*. Why? The name you carry is having effect. The early disciples rejoiced when beaten in Acts 5, because Jesus was showing in their lives.

"When they saw the courage of Peter and John...they took note that these men had been with Jesus." Acts 4:13

The promise of blessing is twofold: a reward is being held in heaven for you and you have become like the prophets of old. It can be said of you as it was said of them:

"You have become the salt of the earth!" Matt 5:13

They are recorded in the annals of time and sit in the cloud of witnesses. Perhaps this is being reserved for us too!

There you are! The nine commanded blessings released by Jesus to the disciples, which means they are open for all who become his servants and disciples.

CHAPTER 16
HOW WE ARE
BLESSED ALONGSIDE ABRAHAM
BLESSED THROUGH FAITH

There are two subjects that I have mentioned throughout this book. Firstly, that we can be blessed alongside Abraham. Secondly, that through our being united to Christ we are released into his blessings (which of course I majored on in Chapter 14). Now comes the verse in Galatians that ties the two blessings together.

> *"He redeemed us in order that the blessing given to Abraham might come to the Gentiles through Christ Jesus, so that by faith we might receive the promise of the Spirit."* Galatians 3:14

Let's look at what this has revealed. God who preordained our blessings did several things. He redeemed us to blessing. He gave us a father of faith to bless us alongside. Of course, he does it all through Christ Jesus who obtained it on our behalf. Then he shows us how to get into this blessing:

> *"So those who rely on faith are blessed along with Abraham, the man of faith."* Galatians 3:9

Like Abraham, we rely on faith. We rely on faith in Christ and his finished work, faith in God's intentions for us, faith in the promises of God toward us and faith in the ability of God, as in Romans.

> *"...being fully persuaded that God had power to do what he had promised."* Romans 4:21

God knows that faith comes from him and he releases promises and encounters so, like Abraham, we can increase in faith and then increase in blessings!

In Genesis 12 God speaks promises to Abraham and then appears to him and speaks to him again and again. In Genesis 14 he appears to him with the bread and the wine. In Genesis 17 he speaks the promise of Isaac. Then he continues to encounter and speak to him, building his faith life. He does no differently with us. He speaks to us through his word, he introduces the Christ to us,

> *"No one can come to me unless the Father who sent me draws them..."* John 6:44

Then he gives us promises and encounters to draw us into the fullness of his blessing.

Now comes the tremendous promise of Galatians 3:14: the promise of the Spirit. When we are touched by faith it opens us to receive the Holy Spirit by faith like the Galatians. Galatians Chapter 3 lights up with this whole subject. Why is it so important? Because he is the revealer of the promises and blessings as is written in Paul's letter to the Corinthians. Take time to read 1 Corinthians 2:9-15.

The revealer is given so that we might see, just like Abraham:

"Whatever you see is yours," Genesis 13:14

The revealer is given so that we might encounter: Ephesians 3:20.

The revealer is given to help us gain our blessings.

"And I will ask the Father, and he will give you another advocate to help you..." John 14:16.

The revealer is given that he might lead us into our blessings,

"For those that are led by the spirit of God are the children of God." Romans 8:14.

THE SPIRIT IS THE BLESSING GIVEN THAT HE MIGHT DIRECT US INTO ALL OUR BLESSINGS. One cannot desire to fathom what kind of touch of the Spirit Abraham actually knew. However deep or personal it was it is for us, too! All of it was planned by God! All of it was walked by Abraham, all gained by Christ and all accessed by the Spirit of God! Just fathomless when you begin to meditate on such a God of blessing and faith!

CHAPTER 17
I HAVE BLESSED HIM AND HE WILL BE BLESSED

Welcome to the words of Isaac to his son Esau:

> *"I blessed him--and indeed he will be blessed!"*
> Genesis 27:33

Jacob had stolen Esau's blessing and Esau wanted it rectified. Isaac said, once I have blessed then he will be blessed. What is this we are seeing? When one who has been blessed by God blesses another the blessing is imparted. Remember that Abraham was told he would be a blessing. Jabez, in his prayer, asked for a double blessing which means he wanted to be able to bless.

Remember again the principle that Jesus gave us:

> *"Freely you have received, freely give."*
> Matthew 18:8

Whatever you receive from God, that you should give. Isaac is blessed twice by God and presumably by Abraham in Genesis 26 because he clearly uses the power to bless. Jacob, too, follows this course in Genesis 49 as he blesses his sons. If blessed by anointing or gifting or whatever, that can be used to bless. Paul spoke of it to Timothy:

> *"Do not neglect your gift, which was given you through prophecy when the body of elders laid their hands on you."* 1 Timothy 4:14

You were imparted to by two things: prophesy and the laying on of hands. A blessing was imputed.

What a tremendous blessing to be used of God to impart his blessings. Once we have received his blessings we should look to be a blessing. Fathers and parents can do it. Anointed ministries can do it. Those carrying God given mantels as Elijah in 1 Kings 19 can do it. Whatever we are blessed with can become a blessing to others.

Listen to the certainty of Isaac's retort: *I have blessed him and he will be blessed.* The imparting of blessing must come with faith from the one imparting. Isaac knew when he blessed that Jacob would be blessed. Faith comes with our blessing but to impart it we must operate in the same faith as when we receive it. Equally, the one receiving the blessing must receive it in the same faith! God uses people as his vessels. We must receive from his people as though he were the one giving. That's why Paul remonstrated with Timothy, *you received it now use it*!

The commanded blessings can be passed on in this realm. The God who sent Jesus to bring many sons to glory wants the sons to share the glory they have received.

CHAPTER 18

BLESSING THOSE THAT ARE BLESSED

It has been mentioned that when the Lord gave Abraham his incredible promise of blessing, he made quite a statement,

> *"I will bless those that bless you and whoever curses you will be cursed,"* Genesis 12:3

Whoa… although the subject of this book is regarding the commanded blessings, what a warning is also given. When we curse a blessed person, it could reverse our own blessing.

To bless one that is blessed is to show honor to them. We can see their obvious blessing and add our blessings to it financially, with words of blessing and honor and whatever we can do to add to their blessing. But how can I tell a man is blessed? I think the children of Heth, the Canaanites show it quite clearly. Abraham asks if he can bury Sarah actually in Hebron which is quite significant.

> *"Hear us, my lord: Thou art a mighty prince among us…" Genesis 23:6* KJV

In other words, they could see who he was! These are Canaanites and they could see. Often throughout the Bible heathen kings and leaders recognized the hand of God and the blessing of God on people. How much more should the Spirit of God within us recognize who is blessed of the

Lord. We don't have to even agree with them or their persuasions but must recognize his blessing!

Cursing one who is blessed is sadly done more often than we realize. The word here means *to make of little account; to slight*. How easy this is to do!

> *"...for their sake he rebuked kings: 'Do not touch my anointed ones; do my prophets no harm.'"* Psalm 105:14-15

While we quote this Psalm and cry of ourselves that one should not touch us, the Lord's anointed, do we in fact do it ourselves to other anointed people? We make light of others' gifts and lives far too easily. We make statements against their style of ministry or their personalities, quote their lack of anointing and look for fault.

We need to make it a habit of blessing ALL those that are blessed in any way of the Lord. This is a wonderful way of gaining a commanded blessing: look for another that is blessed and bless alongside the Lord! Act in agreement with the Lord himself. To be honest it is just a plain Godly way to behave anyway.

> *"Bless those who persecute you; bless and do not curse."* Romans 12:14

That scripture is related to being persecuted. Well then, how much more are we to bless those who are blessed and to agree with God! This opens the windows of blessing so quickly!

CHAPTER 19
IT IS MORE BLESSED TO GIVE THAN TO RECEIVE

Paul, speaking to Ephesian elders, reminds them of what Jesus said,

> *" 'It is more blessed to give than to receive.' "*
> Acts 20:35

Giving is none other than the nature of God.

> *"For God so loved the world that he gave...."*
> John 3:16

God not only *gave* but gave the best. Giving becomes part of the life and nature of being touched by God. Abraham, when he met Melchizedek, instantly gave. Jacob gave, too, when he encountered the Lord in Genesis 28. Giving just plain opens the windows of heaven.

> *" 'Bring the whole tithe into the storehouse, that there may be food in my house. Test me in this,' says the Lord Almighty, 'and see if I will not throw open the floodgates of heaven and pour out so much*

> *blessing that there will not be room enough to store it.' "* Malachi 3:10.

We are told by Jesus himself,

> *"Give and it will be given to you. A good measure, pressed down, shaken together and running over, will be poured into your lap."* Luke 6:38

The verse gives the measure of the blessing. That's a whole lot of blessing! Giving opens the door to all the grace of God.

> *"Each of you should give what you have decided in your heart to give, not reluctantly or under compulsion, for God loves a cheerful giver. And God is able to bless you abundantly, so that in all things at all times, having all that you need, you will abound in every good work."* 2 Corinthians 9:7-8

You don't get higher blessing than that!
You can see that we must give out of a heart of generosity and not begrudgingly because according to this scripture, *"God loves a cheerful giver"*. As in the ways of God, a heart of love is being expressed in giving. Giving truthfully can be about more than just money. It can involve time and any blessings we have! In God's case, he gave his son and once he did that he won't hold anything back! Here is a tremendous scripture:

"He that spared not his own son, but delivered him up for us all, how shall he not with him also freely give us all things?" Romans 8:32 KJV

Giving can cover every dimension of life but it clearly shows us money is involved throughout scripture. In fact, in 2 Corinthians 8, Paul openly boasts of the giving spirit of the Macedonian churches and speaks of their grace of giving. Listen to this last statement in that part of the passage that speaks of giving:

"--see that you also excel in this grace of giving." 2 Corinthians 8:7

Why? Because you reap what you sow according to Galatians:

"Whoever sows to please their flesh, from the flesh will reap destruction; whoever sows to please the Spirit from the Spirit will reap eternal life." Galatians 6:8.

The verse clearly states when it comes to giving, you cannot mock God.

So many scriptures support giving financially. This is quite an intensive subject! God speaks so much about it because he wants you blessed. Multitudes of verses cover tithes and offerings. Both were already mentioned when Malachi 3 was brought up earlier. The Lord says you rob him when you don't give, because you stop him being able to bless in the verses leading up to Malachi 3:10:

> *"Will a mere mortal rob God? Yet you rob me. But you ask, 'How are we robbing you?' In tithes and offerings. You are under a curse—your whole nation—because you are robbing me."* Malachi 3:8-9

David took special offerings for the temple. Offerings can also include offerings for special needs, houses of God or firstfruit offerings:

> *"You are to give them the firstfruits of your corn, new wine and olive oil, and the first wool from the shearing of your sheep..."* Deuteronomy 18:4,

There are also offerings to the poor which hold promises of their own:

> *"Whoever is kind to the poor lends to the Lord, and he will reward them for what they have done."* Proverbs 19:17
> *"The generous will themselves be blessed, for they share their food with the poor."* Proverbs 22:9

> *"Good will come to those who are generous and lend freely, who conduct their affairs with justice."* Psalm 112:5

Generosity comes with salvation, grace and the fear of the Lord. There is a command to it that must not be missed. In fact, I believe we must pray that we become givers so that we can be blessed to give! 2 Corinthians 9:6-13 covers it so well. Verse 11 says that we are so blessed because of our giving that we can give on every occasion. Now here is a blessing indeed:

> *"You will be enriched in every way so that you can be generous on every occasion, and through us your generosity will result in thanksgiving to God."*
> 2 Corinthians 9:11

CHAPTER 20
THE BLESSINGS ON THE HOUSE OF OBED-EDOM

The ark of God in the Old Testament represents the manifested glory of God. This is where he hovered and met the priesthood in the tabernacle.

> *"There, above the cover between the two cherubim that are over the ark of the covenant law, I will meet with you and give you all my commands for the Israelites."* Exodus 25:22

In 1 Samuel chapters 2-4 the story is told of how the Israelites had lost the ark of the covenant due to their wayward priesthood. At the shocking news of the loss, the death of her husband, his brother and Eli the priest, Eli's daughter-in-law died giving birth to a son who was named *Ichabod* meaning *the departing of the glory of God*:

> *"She named the boy Ichabod, saying, 'The Glory has departed from Israel'—because of the capture of the ark of God and the deaths of her father-in-law and her husband. She said, 'The Glory has departed from Israel, for the ark of God has been captured.' "* 1 Samuel 4:21-22

David was desperate for the ark's return but he made a mistake in not seeking the prescribed way it should be carried.

> *"It was because you, the Levites, did not bring it up the first time that the Lord our God broke out in anger against us. We did not enquire of him about how to do it in the prescribed way."*
> 1 Chronicles 15:13.

As a result God showed his displeasure and David had to place the ark in the house of Obed-Edom. He was a priest and would know how to show the right reverence for the presence and Glory of God. For three months the ark remained in his house. Give heed to what happens to Obed-Edom and his house:

> *"The ark of God remained with the family of Obed-Edom in his house for three months, and the Lord blessed his household and everything he had."*
> 1 Chronicles 13:14

Now that sounds like the blessing of God, in a sentence! He and his household and everything he had was blessed simply by housing that which carried the glory of God. The ark, of course, can represent the life of Christ within us because of all that the ark contained. It contained the mercy seat, the covenants of God written by the finger of God, the Holy Spirit himself, Aaron's rod that budded, the favor of God, angels facing one another and the Glory of God resting upon us.

We need the ark of God in our house! Christ in us brings all this ministry of the Lord and causes the glory to rest on us. No wonder the Bible says,

> *"...the commission God gave me to present to you.... the mystery that has been kept hidden for ages and generations, but is now disclosed to the Lord's people...the glorious riches of this mystery, which is Christ in you, the hope of glory."*
> Colossians 2:26-27

When The life of Christ is in residence:

> The mercy seat is manifested in us:
>
> > *"Let us then approach God's throne of grace with confidence, so that we may receive mercy and find grace to help us in our time of need."*
> > Hebrews 4:16.

The word of God is written on our hearts by the Holy Spirit:

> *"You show that you are a letter from Christ, the result of our ministry, written not with ink but with the Spirit of the living God, not on tablets of stone but on tablets of human hearts."* 2 Cor 3:3

His favor is released to us:

> *"I tell you, now is the time of God's favour, now is the day of salvation."* 2 Corinthians 6:2

Angels minister to us:

> *"Are not all angels ministering spirits sent to serve those who will inherit salvations?"* Hebrews 1:14

Carrying Christ in us will bring the blessing of God on us and everything we have. No wonder Joshua made this incredible statement:

> *"But as for me and my household, we will serve the Lord."* Joshua 24:15

I guess he had quickly figured what brings the commanded blessing!

The ark of God remained with the family of Obed-Edom in his house for three months. It was in his house and recorded to be so and manifestly so. Friends, when the ark of the Lord is in your house it's not just your personal house (your life) affected, but your household is affected and everything you have. Everybody knows it's there because it is evident it is there. Let's make room! let's become the hosts of the glory of God! The rest is automatic as his blessing follows his glory!

SUMMARY

As we mentioned in our Introduction and throughout this book, it was God's intention to bless man right from creation. Provision has been made by his commanded blessings throughout the word which we have opened up in all of our chapters. But there is a verse that so sums up these intentions that I wanted to drop it in our summary.

> *"The blessing of the Lord, it maketh rich, and he addeth no sorrow to it."* Proverbs 10:22 KJV

The word used for *rich* in the original language means *to prosper and grow and increase*. It means that the blessing of the Lord enriches in every area of your life. It touches everything. That is the desire that the Lord has for each one of us. What we have done in this book is find some of those areas where the Lord has pre-commanded that blessings will flow. As in everything that is to do with the Bible, the Holy Spirit is ultimately the revealer of truth. He has revealed in his mercy to me a few of those awesome gems. His desire is to prosper you and bless you with all the blessings that he has set aside for you. My honest opinion is that he predestined us for blessing. What father wouldn't? Listen to this great scripture:

> *"Praise be to the God and Father of our Lord Jesus Christ, who has blessed us in the heavenly realms with every spiritual blessing in Christ. For he chose us in him before the creation of the world to be holy and blameless in his sight. In love he predestined us for adoption to sonship through Jesus Christ, in accordance with his pleasure and will."* Ephesians 1:3-5

He blessed us in heavenly places, he chose us before the foundation of the world, and he predestined us to adoption as sons by Jesus Christ to himself. IT WAS ALL PLANNED SO THAT HE COULD BLESS US WITH THE INHERITANCE OF SONSHIP. My friends, grasp what the intentions of the Lord are. Grasp the sonship we gain receiving Jesus Christ. Then let the Holy Spirit awaken us to the preset blessings that our ours.

Surely the Lord has commanded the blessings and they are ours to gain!!!

TESTIMONIALS

"Most of us seek to get the blessing of God on our lives. And it's good that we value it enough to pursue it. We want to please and delights Him and gives Him glory on the earth. And yet, we can pursue His blessing entirely for our own personal reasons. The speaks about "the commanded blessing" and gives us clues of reasons and conditions for which God bestows this blessing. Dennis, a prophet who is also a very gifted Bible teacher, unpacks for us the kind of heart that God is delighted to see and willing to bless. You will enjoy this book. And I think it will help you experience your heart's desire."

Dr. Barry Wissler
President

HarvestNet International
We Fulfill the Great Commission Together

This is a Kingdom book. A much-needed Kingdom book. My friend, Dennis Goldsworthy-Davis masterful work, *Gaining the Command Blessing,* will revolutionize how you think, speak, pray and live. Dennis is a gifted student and teacher of the Word of God. This is demonstrated in his passionate teaching style and in every book he writes. After reading *Gaining the Command Blessing,* you will agree, that the revelation and empowerment held within these pages have the potential to wreck your life (for the good) and position you to live where you were created to live, in His Presence! *Gaining the Command Blessing,* should be on the bookshelf of every leader in all walks of life. Among other things, it's a road map for empowering and releasing the next generation into purpose.
Thank you Dennis for writing this book. We will use it at Kingdom University.

Dr. Greg Hood, Th.D.
Apostolic Leader, Global Reformation Ministries
President, Kingdom University
Author of: *Rebuilding The Broken Altar – Awaking Out Of Chaos*
www.GregHood.org

BIOGRAPHY

Dennis Paul Goldsworthy-Davis has been blessed to travel extensively throughout the world ministering both apostolically and prophetically to the body of Christ. He operates within a strong governmental prophetic office and frequently sees the Presence of God and the Spirit of Revival break out upon the lives of people. Dennis has equally been graced to relate to many spiritual sons throughout the earth, bringing wisdom, guidance and encouragement.

Born in Southern Ireland and raised in England, Dennis was radically saved from a life of drugs and violence in 1973. Soon after his conversion, he began to operate within his local church where he was fathered spiritually by Bennie Finch, a seasoned apostolic minister. After working in youth ministry Dennis pastored in several areas within the U.K. It was during these pastorates that Dennis began to see profound moves of God in these same venues.

In 1986 Dennis experienced a dramatic shift in his life and ministry. He and his family moved to San Antonio, Texas, to join a vibrant, functioning apostolic team.
In 1990 Dennis was commissioned to start Great Grace International Christian Center, a local work in San Antonio. Dennis continues to serve as the Senior /Minister of GGICC and heads the formation of the apostolic team in the local house. Presently, Dennis relates to several functioning apostolic ministries. He draws wisdom and

accountability from Robert Henderson of Global Reformers, Barry Wissler of HarvestNet International and for many years before his passing, Alan Vincent. Each of these carry strong, well-seasoned apostolic offices in their own right.

Dennis has been married to his wife Christine since 1973 and has two wonderful daughters and four grandchildren.

Made in the USA
Middletown, DE
22 February 2022